WITHDRAWN

Like We Say Back Home

Illinois Central College
Learning Resources Center

LIKE WE SAY

BACK HOME

by

Dick Syatt

CITADEL PRESS

Secaucus, N.J.

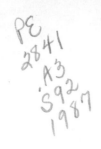

Published 1987 by Citadel Press
A division of Lyle Stuart Inc.
120 Enterprise Ave., Secaucus, N.J. 07094
In Canada: Musson Book Company
A division of General Publishing Co. Limited

This book was originally published in 1980 as *Country Talk.*

Manufactured in the United States of America

ISBN 0-8065-1055-2

LIKE WE SAY BACK HOME

is dedicated to

a very special woman,

MY WIFE, JANE.

There isn't a better wife,
lover, and pal than her.

She's as pretty as a bald-faced heifer

Acknowledgments

This might sound like a poor man's Oscar Award acceptance speech, but there are so many people to thank for their effort. And besides, what is this page for anyway?

A big thank you to Lyle Stuart for taking a chance on this late night talk show host; to the many thousands of contributors who took the time to send in their favorite sayings; to my many colleagues around the country and in Canada, who also took a chance on a novel idea to help write a book, instead of just plugging it:

Larry Kent—WINZ, Miami, Fla.

John Brandmeir—WYBR, Rockford, Ill.

Bob Cudmore—WBEC, Pittsfield, Ma.

Jim White—KMOX, St. Louis, Mo.

David Gilton—WEEI, Boston, Mass.

Dave Newman—WXYZ, Detroit, Mich.

Carol Arnold—KPAC, Port Arthur, Tex.

Ted Barris—CFQC, Canada

Bob Lee—KSL, Salt Lake City, Utah

Dave Stanford—KRMG, Oklahoma

Caroline Jackson—KOBJ, Austin, Tex.

Bob Barry—WEMP, Milwaukee, Wis.

Ed Fisher—WBBG, Cincinnati, O.

Scott Wallace—KPOL, Los Angeles, Calif.

Peter Laufer—KXRX, San Jose, Calif.

Ed Busch—WFAA, Dallas, Tex.

Glenn Ordway—WITS, Boston, Mass.

Nick Anthony—WHLO, Akron, O.

Bill Miller—WGY, Schenectady, N.Y.

Allan Dale—WOAI, San Antonio, Tex.

Steve McFarland—WLW, Cincinnati, O.

Bob Massey—WKRG, Mobile, Ala.

Milton Metz—WHAS, Louisville, Ky.

Rick Cummings—WTIC, Hartford, Conn.

There were other radio shows and newspaper coverage, but space is limited and a big thank you to all.

Two years ago, when I was in Dallas, astrologer Jack Gillen from Orlando, Florida, told me that I would be writing a book. At that time I told him he was nuts. . . . Well, he may still be nuts, but the book is written. I thank Jack for his support and guidance.

I would also like to thank my father for his ability to be a friend, sounding board, punching bag, and devoted father.

And the biggest acknowledgment to my mother, Selma, for living above and beyond the call of duty as a mother, friend and partner.

CONTENTS

FOREWORD

On a windy, cold, west Texas Sunday afternoon in January, after my good friend Dick Syatt told me on the phone from Boston that he was going to make a book of his incredible collection of homespun sayings, I lifted a big mesquite log onto the dying coals in my fireplace, took another chew of tobacco and sat back to think about his project.

Like a dream, in panorama, I envisioned a kaleidoscope of peoples from untold generations and diverse nationalities, from all regions of our great country, who made it possible for Dick's book to become a reality.

In my mind's eye I could see immigrants from Western European countries moving past the Statue of Liberty and through the lines at Ellis Island; Asians and Pacific island natives passing under the Golden Gate Bridge; cowpunchers and sheepherders from the slopes of the Rocky Mountains; California gold miners; Mexican vaqueros from the Sonora and Chihuahua desert expanses; coal diggers from the Appalachians; wheat farmers from the prairie states; hog growers of the Midwest; apple pickers from the Northwest; steelworkers from the environs of the Great Lakes; Okie dust bowl drifters; Louisiana cajuns; Georgia crackers; Tennessee moonshiners; Cape Cod fisherfolk; Mississippi river rats; old soldiers from San Juan Hill; Nevada gamblers; Texas dancehall girls; preachers in old brush arbor meetings; bums on half a hundred big city skid rows; and a multitude of just plain, common folks, mostly like you and me, all who have either created from their fertile imaginations or have developed from their bountiful experiences certain sayings or regional words of wisdom that have become colorful expressions of true Americanism. Can we call them sage sayings by the souls of the sod and the sea?

In an earlier day, a popular saying was: "Sharper than the serpent's tooth is the thankless child." Before that one came along, or soon after, we heard: "A whistling girl and a crowing hen is neither good to God or men, and always comes to some bad end." These gems carry a message that is as good today as it was the day they were first uttered, as does the old adage: "A man convinced against his will is of the same opinion still."

Edgar A. Guest passed to us such sage advice as, "It takes a heap of livin' to make a house a home." Yarn-spinning, rope-twisting Oklahoman Will Rogers is best known for: "I never met a man I didn't like."

So, from earliest time right up to today we have had folks give us advice and knowledge in the form of sayings or regionalisms. Dick Syatt has mixed for us a bountiful bowl of some of the best expressions that have come down the pike. I like to think of Dick's work as a "Book of Proverbs," because

"A proverb is a sacred relic; a short saying spoken after long experience—a tiny crystal left after lengthy evaporation."

Jerry Mack Johnson
San Angelo, Texas

Author of:
Country Wisdom
Catfish Farming
Country Scrapbook
Down Home Ways

INTRODUCTION

As I sit in my apartment in downtown Boston, overlooking the Prudential Building to my right, the new John Hancock Tower to my left, and the manuscript of *Country Talk* in my lap, I can't help but marvel at the way this project came about.

As a transplanted Yankee living in Texas, I fell in love with the lifestyle, the warmth of the people, and the expression of the Southwest. I was hosting the early evening telephone talk show in Dallas, at WFAA Radio, and came in contact with people from every corner of the Mid- and Southwest.

One evening I was searching for something new and different to talk about on the show (don't let me kid you . . . this happened all the time). I knew that Texans loved to talk about their homeland, so I asked the listeners to phone in with their favorite homespun sayings, phrases, and "Texanisms." The response was breathtaking! They loved it.

For four hours listeners phoned in, and did we laugh, cry, and giggle! That night I suggested that we should make this "our" project, and write a book together—actually compile a collection of sayings and submit it as a collaboration of a talk show host and his listeners. I received mail, from my listeners, by the hundreds. We repeated the show again and again, and the response grew.

A few agents and publishers were contacted, but the response was a bit less than encouraging. There didn't seem to be a market for our project. I shelved the idea, and turned my attention to other things. When we were packing to return to Boston, I threw away all the material for the book, but at the last moment, I pulled it out of the trash—"just in case."

In Boston now, I'm hosting the late night talk show, and my guest for the night is Lyle Stuart, in to discuss his latest book, *Casino Gambling for the Winner*. During one of the newscast breaks, I mentioned the collection of sayings to Lyle. One thing led to another, and within weeks I began searching for sayings from around the country.

When it came to collecting the sayings, I did not want to rely on dusty old books in libraries, or on old magazine articles dated 1936. Instead, I decided to use the method I knew best—talk shows.

I got in touch with fifty or sixty of the leading talk show hosts from California to Maine and Canada. They were very interested in the project, and the response from their listeners was just as great as it was in Dallas. As a matter of fact, we repeated many of the shows.

You might think, as I did before the search began, that each section of the country would have phrases, expressions and sayings that are unique to them. What I found to be true was quite the opposite. Many of the sayings I had heard in Texas or Kansas were repeated to me in Boston or California. There may have been a very slight variation, but for the most part, I felt that they could be traced to a common origin.

One thing to keep in mind is the effect of the modern media in spreading the word. Think about it . . . there really are very few small out-of-the-way communities and towns, as we knew them years ago. Today our society

is extremely mobile, with most Americans uprooting
themselves at least eleven times in a lifetime. Even those
people who live and die in rural America travel more,
or are at least more aware of their world than ever before
as a result of exposure to radio and TV.

So, when grandma or grandpa coined a phrase when
the cow jumped clear over the fence, or put down Sally's
ugly face, it spread like wildfire. There have been a few
attempts to trace the origins of the sayings, but I think
Alex Hailey's next project ought to be to trace the roots
of an expression to its ancestors and follow its path
through the country.

I didn't want *Country Talk* to resemble an encyclopedia
of the history of sayings, or to present itself as a "com-
plete" collection of sayings and phrases. Instead, I saw
Country Talk as an entertaining collage of the most
widely used and popular expressions. That is why I asked
people from all over the country to contribute their
favorites, the ones they use on a day-to-day basis.

I have categorized *Country Talk* into several areas
dealing with everything from age, anger and love to hate,
putdowns, compliments and phrases for every occasion.
So, if you want to be able to spice up your vocabulary
with some grass roots talk, or just want a chuckle, you
can pick up *Country Talk* and select a phrase or two.

You will notice names under some of the sayings.
That's because I offered name credit to anyone sending in
a contribution. Actually there should be thousands of
names, but due to space and some duplication, we had to
limit name credit to those received first for a particular
word or phrase, or the most original. The names listed
do *not* indicate the originator of a saying, poem, or expression.

It was very difficult to set a cutoff point for completion
of this book, because every time I thought that we were
ready, many more contributions came in. I hope that if
you have any favorite expressions or sayings, you will jot
them down and send them to me in care of the publisher.
They may be included in the next edition.

The address is toward the back of the book, under "Write Your Own." In this chapter, you are provided space to make a list of your own personal or family gems.

Above all else, just kick off your shoes, and enjoy *Country Talk!*

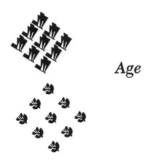

Age

AS OLD
AS THE HILLS

Age is a matter of mind. If you don't mind, it doesn't matter.

Mildred Hankin, Milwaukee, Wisconsin

Don't let age become your cage.

Toni Cowan, San Antonio, Texas

A woman who tells her age will tell everything.

He's just climbing up fool's hill [*Meaning a youngster*].

He's not dry behind the ears [*Meaning young and inexperienced*].

Gordon Baird, Whitesboro, New York

You look like a million . . . every year of it.

Forty is the old age of youth; fifty is the youth of old age.

Mrs. Sharon Smith, Wisconsin

19

Why, you old snuff-dipper, you!

If you want to know, ask old numbnuts over thar!

He's so stubborn, we just call him old iron ass.

Why, he's as old as the hills!

If you need an old and experienced person for a job, you might need "An old dog for a hard road."
Ray Mickers, Louisville, Kentucky

He's been around longer than dirt!

That ole salty buzzard's been around for many a year.
John and Floy Benson, Desoto, Texas

Old Henry is so old, he could have been a waiter at the Last Supper.

I cain't jump that rope. I'm no spring chicken!

I'm too old a cat to be fooled by a kitten. [A man to his son]
Edward N. Hytinen, Milwaukee, Wisconsin

I'm looking 'round the clock. [Looking old]

As old as my tongue and a little older than my teeth. [Answer to "How old are you?"]

He's been here since Dewey was a midshipman.

When your children are small they step on your toes. When they grow up, they step on your heart.
Jeanine Mazynski   and   Mrs. James Gauthier,
Caledonia, Wisconsin   Wisconsin

20

Anger

HE'S HOPPIN' MAD

He's so nasty that when he's in the hospital the nurses send him get well cards.

He's out of snuff. *[Upset, in Texas]*

Oh! He's hoppin' mad!

Zelma Martin

He flew off the handle again last night.

He hit the ceiling.

He's all bent out of shape.

She's madder than a wet hen without a roost.

He's mad enough to chew splinters.

His back is up over what she did.

His nose is out of joint. *[Upset and jealous]*

He told him how the cow ate the cabbage. *[He told him a thing or two]*

23

C❖C❖C❖C❖C❖C❖C❖C❖C❖C❖C❖C❖C❖C❖

He cleaned his plow. *[He beat him up, Texas]*

He'll jump on you faster than a duck on a June bug.

She made me so mad, I ran a sugar ant through a picket fence and stomped a dead chicken!

Get out of my way or I'll hit you so hard that your dress will fly up your back like a window shade!

There aren't many people I would kick in this world. You're an exception.

I'll hit you with so many rights, you'll scream for a left.

I'll put the strap to you. *[Hit with a razor strop]*

I'm so angry, I'm ready to fling a Joe Blizzard fit!

I'm so irritated, I could go to pot and buy a skillet.

My back hairs sure riz when I heard that.

I'll slap you bald-headed if I hear of you doin' that again.

I'm gonna be on him, like a South Texas wind!

George Cofer, Jr.

I'm so mad, I could chew nails and spit spikes!

I'm gonna frail the hell out of ya!

I'm still in a pucker over what he did to me last year.

Ruth Lyon, Augusta, Maine

I'll turn you every way but loose.

Paul Gustafson, Austin, Texas

When I get him cornered, I'm gonna make the fur fly.

If you don't watch it, I'll knock you plumb into next week.

See this finger
See this thumb
See this fist,
You'd better run.

Florence Sokol, Milwaukee, Wisconsin

What's the matter, did you sit on a rabbit? *[Have you got a hair in your behind?]*

Now wouldn't that rattle your slats and walk on your plaster?

Marge Harkness, Clifton Park, New York

Now don't get your tail over the dash. *[Don't be upset]*

Now don't get your tail up over your back.

It's enough to make a preacher lay his Bible down.

Mrs. A. Prince, Troy, Texas

You're achin' for a breakin', if you keep that up.

You're stinkin' for a whippin'.

He's hurtin' for certain.

That ol' boy is aimin' for a maimin'.

If you keep that up, you'll be cruisin' for a bruisin'.

He's on the list for my fist.

If you don't stop, you'll be eating a knuckle sandwich.

Your mother is gonna tan your fanny if you don't stop.

Don't bust your bloomers, girl, it'll be all right.

Gol dang it, girl—don't do that again.

Take a long walk on a short pier.
M. Templeman, East Otis, Massachusetts

Get off my tail, you're walking too close.

OK, boys, quit that fightin' and scratchin'.

Go fry some ice.
M. Strasnick, Lynn, Massachusetts

Go fry a snowball.

I'm as mad as fire.

To hell I pitch it! *[To hell with it, Nova Scotia]*

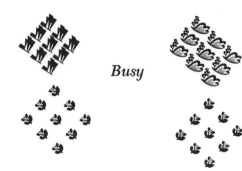

Busy

BUSY AS A BEE
IN A BASIN

27

She busier than a cat in a tripe shop.

That man is busier than a cranberry merchant at Thanksgiving.

He's busier than a cat on a marble-topped table.
Bette S. Allen, Canton, Pennsylvania

She's as busy as a bee in a basin.

That ole girl is as busy as a pregnant squirrel in a forest fire.
Helen Roach, Salem, Ohio

He's busier than a tick in a tea bucket.

He's busier than a one-armed paper hanger with the hives during strawberry season.

He's busier than someone with a seven-year itch and an eight-day clock. When he ain't scratchin', he's windin' the clock.

He's busier than a pair of jumper cables at a family picnic.
Selma Morrison, Lynn, Massachusetts

He's running on one foot.
F. G., Marblehead, Massachusetts

I can't take long—I have to get back to my rat-killing. *[Referring to "busy work"]*
Al Past, Beeville, Texas

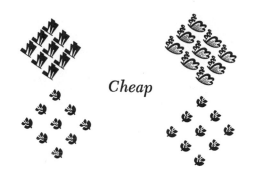

Cheap

HE SQUEAKS
WHEN HE WALKS

He's so cheap that he squeezes a dollar till the eagle hollers.

He's as tight as Dick's hatband.

He's so tight that he squeaks when he walks.

He's as tight as a fiddlestring.

She's as tight as a clothesline.

He's so stingy that he crawls under the gate to save the hinges.

He has short arms and long pockets.

If he had the flu, he wouldn't give you a sneeze.

He's tighter than bark on a tree.

He's as tight as a frog's hind end.

He's tighter than a gnat's ass.

He could squeeze a nickel till the buffalo hollers.

He makes a nickel go so far the buffalo gets sore feet.

She's so cheap she won't take a cold shower because the goose pimples are hard on the soap.

He's tighter than a wet boot.

He will skin a flea for its hide and tallow.

He's so cheap he wouldn't spend a penny to see an earthquake.

She's as stingy as satin.

He is so tight he can sit down on a dime and you can read "In God We Trust" around him.

A BIRD NEVER FLIES SO HIGH BUT WHAT IT HAS TO COME BACK TO THE GROUND FOR SOMETHING TO EAT.

IT'S NOT THE COUGH THAT CARRIES YOU OFF, IT'S THE COFFIN THEY CARRY YOU OFF IN.

Clothes

DRESSED FIT TO KILL

She's dressed fit to kill.

She's dressed up in her Sunday-go-to-meetin' clothes.

You look like somebody come.

He's dressed up like a Philadelphia lawyer.

He's dressed like he just stepped out of the bandbox.
Mary Jo Yanchick

All dressed up like a country bride.
Helen R. Wolf, Louisville, Kentucky

She looks like an old ewe dressed like a lamb.

She's all laid out like a lamb and sallet [salad]. *[Wearing fancy clothes]*

He looks as fine as a new-scraped carrot. *[All dressed up]*

39

That jerk looks like a sow with side pockets. *[Dressed absurdly]*

Her clothes sit on her like a saddle on a sow's back.

The shirt's OK, but your legs are a little long.

She puts her bra on backwards and it fits.

Peggy, Lowell, Massachusetts

She looks like she threw her clothes in the air and ran under them.

That dress shows lovin' hands at home.

She looks as tacky as a scarecrow's offspring in those clothes.

He's all gussied up.

He's all dressed up and nowhere to go.

He's all pissed up and nothing to show.

Go dress your feet and put on your shoes.

*WHEN YOU SPIT UP, IT ALWAYS FALLS
BACK IN YOUR FACE.* [*Advice to a gossiper*]

*A MAN OF WORDS, AND NOT OF DEEDS
IS LIKE A GARDEN FULL OF WEEDS.*

*IF WISHES WERE FISHES
WE'D ALL HAVE SOME FRY
AND IF HORSE TURDS WERE BISCUITS,
WE'D EAT TILL WE DIE.*

Country
Comparisons

GREEN AS A GOURD

As alike as two peas in a pod.

He was all over the place like a chicken with its head cut off.

As mad as a pig on ice with his tail froze in.
                    Mrs. C. H. Gasner, San Antonio

Bitter as gall.

Black as the king of Hell's riding boots.

Blacker than the bottom of a dry hole well at midnight.

She's as blind as a bat.

He's bold as brass.

That boy is as bright as a new penny.

{◇{◇{◇{◇{◇{◇{◇{◇{◇{◇{◇{◇{◇{◇

That's burnt blacker than a crow.
Esther Austin, Augusta, Maine

She's as cautious as a prostitute at confession.

She's as changeable as the wind.

That boy's clean as a whistle.

That floor is clean as print.

That's clear as a bell.

That's clear as glass.

That was closer than the hair on the skin of a chicken's tooth.

He's as clumsy as a bull in a china closet.

Oh, that's as common as pig tracks.
Beverly Nix Coiner, San Antonio, Texas

As common as a belly button—everybody's got one.

That's as common as cat shit, and twice as nasty.

She covered him like the dew covers Dixie.
J. W. Waggoner, San Antonio

I'm as confused as a cat on a hot tin roof.

That ol' girl's as crazy as a loon.

As crazy as a bullbat.

He's as crazy as Laraby's calf.

He's crazier than a backhouse rat.

That guy is crookeder'n a dog's hind legs.

He's as crooked as a snake.

He's as crooked as a barrel of fish hooks.
Gladys Bradford, Erwin, Tennessee

He's as crooked as a corkscrew.

That baby is as curious as a cat.

She's as cute as a kitten—on down south.

The baby is as cute as a speckled pup.

He's as cute as a button.

It's dark as pitch.

It's dark as a black cow's skin.

Dazed as a goose with a nail in its head.
Jerry Mack Johnson

Dazed as a duck in thunder.

He's as dead as a doornail.

He's deader than a hammer.

That ol' girl's deaf as a post.

They're all dressed up like gals going to meeting.

I'm as dry as a powder house. *[Thirsty]*

That party was as dull as a hoe.
Mrs. Dorothy Mankers, Williamstown, Massachusetts

47

He's dumb like a fox.

I'm feeling fair to middlin'.

You're as fine as split silk.

You look fit as a fiddle.

A flat-chested woman is like a bed without a pillow.

He's as foolish as a bag of chaff with the bottom end out.

That young'un is as freckled as a guinea egg.

I feel as fretful as a bear with a toothache.

She's as friendly as a bramble bush.

The puppy's as frisky as a flea on a flat dog.
                                        David Hall, Sherman, Texas

He's as greedy as a fox in a henhouse.

The girl is green as a gourd when it comes to love.

He has a grin like a Cheshire cat chewing on a piece of cheese.

He's grinning like a mule eating cockleburs.

That man is grinning like a mule eating cactus.

He's grinning like a skunk eating cabbage.

He's as handy as a gimlet.

As hard as a lightard knot.

It's as hard as a ground toad.

He's raising more hell than an alligator in a dry lake.

That boy is raising more hell than a pig caught under a gate.

That dress is higher than a cat's back. *[Expensive]*

That boy is hopping like cold water in a hot skillet.

They're jumpier than a truckload of starving kangaroos.

I feel as keen as a briar.

He's as lazy as Uncle Deal.

He's as lazy as a pet coon.

This feels as light as a feather.

This job was like lickin' honey off a thorn. *[Unprofitable]*

She looks as limber as an old dishrag.

He's as lonely as a gander at settin' time.

Man, this seems like it's been longer than a wet week.

It's been longer than a month of Sundays since I've seen you.

He's lower than a snake's bottom on a wagon track.

It was mashed flatter than a fritter.
Roy Parker, Corpus Christi, Texas

That ol' boy's mean as a skunk.

She's as mean as a two-stingered wasp.

He's as mean as sin.

He's meaner than a junkyard dog with fourteen sucking pups.

He's meaner than turkey turd beer.

She's meaner than sour owl urine.

He has a memory like a frog's tail.

That's as mild as a moonbeam.

Billy's as nearsighted as a mole.

It's noisier in here than a cornhusk mattress.
James A. Osterhout, Central Bridge, New York

She don't look good. She's as pale as a ghost.

It's so hot, I'm panting like a lizard on a hot rock.

I'm feeling as pert as a cricket.

He's as phoney as a three-dollar bill.

She's as plain as a pack rat.

She's as popular as a turd in a punch bowl.

That went over like a pregnant bullfrog.

That's like a pump without a handle.

That's as tough as puttin' socks on a rooster.

She's as quiet as a mouse around hungry cats.

That's as rare as a virgin in a cathouse.

50

Why, that's as rare as hen's teeth.

That's as rare as a black cow with a white face.

That's as red as a robin's breast.

That's redder than a turkey's rump at pokeberry time.

Right as rain.

It's rough as sandpaper.

It's rough as a cob.

It's round as a rolypoly.

That's like a round peg in a square hole.

It's as safe as granny's snuff box in her apron pocket.

He's as serious as a jackass in a graveyard.
                    David Hassler, New Braunfels, Texas

He's as sharp as a rubber tack.

That's as profitable as shearin' a pig.

He's as shifty as a barrelful of snakes.

She's as shy as a violet.

She's like a sick kitten on a hot rock. *[Cuddly]*

He's sicker than a mule.

He's just sittin' there like a toad on a shovel.

He's sittin' there like a toad on a stump.

51

He went there as slick as a physic through a goose.

That's as slick as a wax snake on a marble floor.

He's as slick as owl's grease.

That's slicker than a cat's meow.

That's slicker than owl doodoo on a hickory limb.

That's slicker than a boiled onion.

That's slicker than snot on a doorknob.

He's slipperier than a pocket full of custard.

She's as sly as a fox.

It smells like an acre of onions.

That's as smooth as a snake's belly.

That's as smooth as a mole's titty.

That's smoother than silk on a cornstalk.

She's as snug as a rabbit in a fur-lined burrow.
The Marcellus Family, Gloversville, New York

It's as special as a city slicker in his hootenanny.

He's as soft-hearted as a weasel. _[Hard-hearted]_

It's as soft as a butterfly's belly.

It's as soft as a grape.

It's as soft as a two-minute egg.

She's softer than a moth's nose.

Gail Morrison, Berkeley, California

He's got 'em stirred up like a hornet's nest.

He's as strong as Samson.

You are as stubborn as a cross-eyed mule.

You're as subtle as a hollyhock hedge around an outhouse.

He's as subtle as a rhinoceros in heat.

He's as subtle as a garlic sandwich.

She's as subtle as a train wreck.

She's as sweet as baby's breath.

It's as sweet as a rose between two thorns.

It's as sweet as a maiden's kiss.

It's sweeter than an old maid's dream.

He takes to it like a cat goes for clabber.

He takes to you like a hog after persimmons.

He takes to it like a fish to water.

It's as tender as an old maid's heart.

They're as thick as hair on a hog.

It's as thick as mud.

It's tighter than a bull's mouth in fly time.

53

It fits tighter than a skin on a sausage.
Flo, "Alice" Show, CBS-TV

It's tighter than a tick's hatband.

It's as tough as white leather. *[Very strong leather]*

That's tough as a boot.

That's tougher than a stewed owl.

Thats tougher than a piece of whang.

It's tougher than leather spaghetti.

It's warm as toast.

It's as wide as two ox handles and a chaw of tobaccee.

The kids wiggled like a handful of worms in a bed of hot ashes.

She's wilder than a Christmas goose.
Clara Gillespie, Sagamore Hill, Ohio

She's as wild as an acre of snakes.
Ginny Cook, Dallas, Texas

Compliments

THE CAT'S MEOW

He doesn't let grass grow under his feet.

Bless your little cotton socks.

I wouldn't trade you for an acre of pregnant red hogs.

You're a smart cookie.

He's smarter than a hooty owl.

Ellie McKamy, Dallas, Texas

He's as smart as a tree full of owls.

He's as smart as a whip.

She's as sharp as a weasel.

You're a real doozie.

He doesn't have a lazy bone in his body.

You're as bright as a head of cabbage in a pumpkin field.

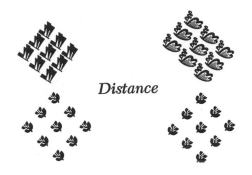

Distance

DOWN THE
ROAD A PIECE

It's where the streetcar bends the corner round.
Steve Karner, Milwaukee, Wisconsin

It's not very far . . . just a look and a holler away.

Just start walkin' . . . it's a far piece.

I won't say it's far, but I had to grease my wagon wheels
three times to get to the main road.

I'm so far south they call people from Georgia Yankees.

I could stretch a mile if I wouldn't have to walk back.
John Kleinowski, Franklin, Wisconsin

The schoolhouse is just a jump away.
Elizabeth Warren, Tulsa Oklahoma

The store is just a hoot and a holler away.
Lois Peck, Pompano Beach, Florida

61

The next town is so far away it's nearly out of this world.

That's higher than a cat's back.

There's no room in here to swing a cat.

We'll be back . . . we're goin' down yonder.

Oh, it's only a short piece to the farmhouse.

It's a wagon-greasin' down the road. *[A great distance]*

I'm fixin' to go down the road a piece. *[A short distance]*

It's longer than a West Kansas well rope. *[Very long]*
      Dick McGuinn, Pawnee County, Oklahoma

Punch my hole in the transfer for a little longer. I wanna go off by Schusters.
      Marge Czecholinski, Muskego, Wisconsin

GIVE A MAN A FISH AND HE WILL EAT FOR A DAY. TEACH HIM HOW TO FISH AND HE WILL EAT FOR A LIFETIME.

Drunk

WET
YOUR WHISTLE

Don't chop no wood. Father's coming home with a load.
Eileen Prondzinski, Wisconsin

Have a drink and wet your whistle.

He's tighter than a Teddy bear.
Jill Coitrone, Augusta, Maine

He's as drunk as a monkey.

He's as stewed as a fresh boiled owl.

He's as drunk as a skunk in a trunk.

He's drunker than Cooter Brown.
Anne Frazor, Weatherford, Texas

You got her drunk, you take her home.

He's four sheets to the wind.

He's 45 degrees listed.

H. Healey, Hobart, New York

Have a hair of the dog that bit ye. *[A hangover remedy]*

I saw him in the bar last night drunker than who shot John.

Al Past, Beeville, Texas

Name your poison.

Your eyes look like two cherries in a bowl of buttermilk.

Your eyes are as red as two cherries in the snow.

We were over-served. *[Excuse for overdrinking]*
John Schmeil, Milwaukee, Wisconsin

I'm so depressed, I'm trying to put out a fire with gunpowder.

Your eyes look like two burned holes in a blanket.

Don't drink more than you can walk out with.
Peg Doersam, Springfield, Massachusetts

Everyday
Exclamations

I'LL BE
HORNSWOGGLED

Well, I'll be dog!

That'll be the frosty Friday before I help him!

Well, shoot a bug!

Bonnie Lee Haynie, Texas

Ye gods and little fishes.

Marc Owen

That's two different buckets of possums! *[Two different stories]*

Albert Lee Wilson, Frankfort, Kentucky

He reminds me of a calf staring at a new gate.

It reminds me of the time that it was so dark I had to light a second match to see if the first one was lit!

Harold M. Rawlinson, Prince Albert, Canada

Stop snapping my garter! *[Pulling my leg]*

I'm telling you, it was so quiet, you could almost hear your hair grow.

I've got to make hay while the sun shines.

He was so mad, he shot that dog graveyard dead.

There she stood, as nekkid as a jaybird.

For pity Moses, stop making all that noise.

My purse is so heavy, I must have everything in here but the cow and the calf.

Great gobs of galloping goose hair!

Oh fiddlesticks in August!

Aw, fiddle britches and Tom Jones!

Aw, sniddle Fritzes.

Man, ain't she a whingdinger!

Jumpin' Jehoshaphat!

Well, flip my garter!

Oh, for garden seed!

Well, I'll be switched!

I really don't give a hoot.

Henry, I don't care if it harelips every cow in Texas!

I'd know his old hide in a tanning yard.

I'd just as soon eat a bug. [Said about something you don't want to do]

Man, I'm snake-bit on this job. [Things going wrong]

Thank you till you're better paid.

My tongue got caught in my eyeteeth and I couldn't see what I was saying.

Get onto yourself and ride the jackass. [Get off your behind]

Max Syatt, Massachusetts

I'll give you twenty lashes of a pussycat's tail.

Mrs. Jack Laurence, San Antonio, Texas

That's so crazy, it would make a stuffed bird laugh.

That money is burning a hole in your pocket.

That's a real barn-burner.

Pat Dollar, Texas

Great gobs of goose grease!

Put that in your pipe and smoke it!

What the Sam Hill! [Expressing surprise]

Well, don't that tear the plank off the house!

I'd walk ten miles over busted beer bottles to get to it.

I feel so low I could jump off a dime.

71

Quit your grinnin' and drop your linen. *[Take your clothes off!]*

Steve Krueger, Dallas, Texas

It's enough to gag a gnat.

Ann Bullard, Broken Arrow, Oklahoma

Don't be such a buttinsky.

Don't rush me, I wasn't born in a day.

Go peddle your own grapes. *[To a meddler]*

I feel lower than a gopher hole.

I feel so low, I could walk under the rug and not cause a ripple.

John D. Morrison, Lynn, Massachusetts

I had a high-helled time last night. *[A good time]*

I haven't had so much fun since the legs fell off my hamster.

Well, cut off my legs and call me shorty!

He's got more money than Carter's got liver pills.

Richard Pitts, Garland, Texas

Good golly, Miss Polly! *[Startled]*

Oh lawsy, miz Agnes! *[Startled]*

Well, I'll be doggone!

Well, I'll be hornswoggled!

I just reckon as how there's a whole heap of old-timey sayings I cain't rightly reckylect.

MY HEAD IS ROUND, MY BODY SMALL.
I LOVE THE BOYS, GOD BLESS THEM
ALL.

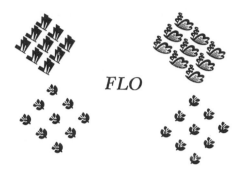

FLO

Polly Holliday, who stars as Flo, the sassy, warm hearted waitress on "Alice" on CBS Television, was born in Jasper, Alabama. Flo uses homespun sayings constantly, and I was delighted when she sent me several of her favorite to use in the book.

Kiss my grits.

He doesn't know diddly squat.

He took her right to the pea patch.

It's none of your beeswax.

It scared the puddin' out of me.

I feel like I've been rode hard and put up wet.

He's working without a full string of lights.

She's got a burr in her saddle.

He's a horse's patoot.

He's as nervous as a long-tailed cat in a room full of rocking chairs.

Tattletale, Tattletale, hang your britches on a nail.

I'm gonna clean your clock. *[Get even]*

He had to go and open his big bazoo.

Put the kibosh on that.

I HAVEN'T BEEN KISSED IN SO LONG I DIDN'T REMEMBER IF YOU SUCK YOUR BREATH IN OR LET IT OUT.
Minnie Pearl

Food

SLOPPIN' GOOD GRAVY

A minute in the mouth, two hours in the stomach, and forever on the lips.

This fried chicken is so good it'll make your teeth white, your skin tight, and childbirth a pleasure.

I could eat her cooking till the cows come home.

That was so good, it would make your tongue slap your brains out!

That tastes good enough to lap your lip over.

That grub is so bad it would hare-lip a dog.
                                    Dona Mileski, Kent, Ohio

That meat was so tough we had to cut the gravy.
                        Charlene Schutz, New Berlin, Wisconsin

Her cooking is so bad it's enough to gag a maggot.

The coffee was so weak I had to help it out of the pot.

That coffee was so strong it would raise a blood blister on a rawhide boot.

The coffee was so strong it could have stood alone.
                                    Ruth Lyon, Augusta, Maine

A biscuit ought to be big enough so that you can't stick out your pinkie to hold it.

When the pig is full, the swill is sour.
                          Mrs. Earle Lever, Rensselaer, New York

I'm not a fast cook, I'm not a slow cook, I'm a half-fast cook.

I always call my Thanksgiving turkey Napoleon, because I like to pick his Bonaparte.
                        Mrs. Allen Krank, Helenville, Wisconsin

Eat all you can and can what you can't.

I could take up the slack of my belly and wipe me eyes with it. *[Very hungry]*

I'm so hungry my belly thinks my throat is cut.

I'm so empty I can feel my backbone touching my belly button.

I'm hungrier than a weasel in a henhouse.

I'm so hungry I'll eat anything that isn't moving.

I'm as hungry as a moth on a nylon sweater.

I'm as hungry as a wolf.

I'm as hungry as a June crow.

I'm as hungry as a grizzly bear.

I've got a honin' for a hog jowl and turnip greens.

I'll eat anything that doesn't eat me first.
Florence Glazner, Dallas, Texas

Poor little young'un, he's starvin' for spoon-fed vittles.
[Grandmother watching her grandson nursing]
Jessie S. Knott, Mayfield, New York

When the mouse gets full the grain gets better.
Mrs. Albert Geise, Brown Deer, Wisconsin

No thank you. At the moment, I'm sufferin' with comfort, and damn sure enjoying my misery! *[After too much to eat]*

My sufficiency is quite suffonsified and more would be an abundance to the superfluity of my obnoxious case.

I has had a genteel sufficiency. Any more would be a vulgar plenty.
H. Healey, Hobart, New York

I'm as full as a stuffed tick on a fat hog.

A full belly makes a dull brain.

My shirt, shimmies and pants are full so I don't care for any more.

I'm as full as an egg.

I'm goin' to make groceries, so that I can take some home and save them. *[Pennsylvania Dutch for going shopping]*
Mrs. Donna B. Coons, Metairie, Louisiana

Don't eat yourself full, Pop, there's pie back yet.
Mrs. John Ebner, Louisville, Kentucky

Aunt Emmy's shoofly pie sure eats good—ain't?
Pennsylvania Dutch

Turn down the spider, the meat is catching down. *[Lower the heat, the meat is burning]*
Mrs. Pat Watson, Wisconsin

This pepper is as hot as ackaforts.

Slap a dollop of lard in the skillet.

How about a mug-up? *[Fisherman talk for coffee break]*

That sure is sloppin' good gravy. *[Good food in Texas]*

Funny

A REAL BLINGER

The first time I heard that, I laughed so hard I kicked a slat out of my crib.

Well now, ain't that a knee-slapper!
Margaret Sieckmann, Milwaukee, Wisconsin

That's more fun than a barrel of monkeys.

That's enough to make a cat laugh.

That's as funny as a crutch.

You're not funny. It's just the way your mother dresses you.
William J. LaVallee, Gloversville, New York

That's as funny as a fart in a space suit.

That's as funny as a rubber crutch.

He couldn't see a joke except by appointment and he'd be late for that.

That's a real blinger! *[Thigh-slapper]*
Ruth, Brookline, Massachusetts

GRANDMOTHER'S RECEET

1. Bild a far in back yard to het kettle of rain-water.

2. Set tubs so smoke won't blow in eyes, if wind is peart.

3. Shave one hole cake of lie sope in biling water.

4. Sort things in three piles—1 pile white, 1 pile cullards, 1 pile work britches and rags.

5. Stur flower in cold water to smooth, then thin down with biling water to make starch.

6. Rub dirty spots on board, scrub hard then bile. Rub cullards, but don't bile, just rench and starch.

7. Take white things out of kettle with broom-stick handle, then rench, blew and starch.

8. Spread tee towels on grass.

9. Hang old rags on fence.

10. Pour rench water in flower beds.

11. Scrub porch with hot sopy water.

12. Turn tubs upside down.

13. Go put on clean dress, smooth hair with side combs, brew cup of tea, set and rest and rock a spell and count blessin's.

Author unknown; submitted by M. Carl, Tupelo, Mississippi

Happy

HAPPY AS A CLAM

87

I haven't had so much fun since pussy was a cat.

I haven't had so much fun since the hogs ate up my little brother.

If I felt any better, I'd think it was a frame-up.

I haven't had so much fun since grandpappy caught his head in Sonny's electric train.

Minnie Pearl

I'm as happy as a jackass eating sawbriars.

Ed Skaggs, Texas

I'm as happy as a clam at high tide.

I'm as happy as a pig in a hog-woller.

Jerry Mack Johnson

I'm as happy as a pig in the sunshine.

I'm happier than a rabbit in a carrot patch.

I'm as pleased as a dog waggin' two tails.

I'm as contented as a cow in a corn patch.

I'm as happy as a hog with his head in a slop bucket.

I'm as happy as a pig in clover.

I'm as happy as a pig in mud.
Yvonne Steiman, Charlestown, Massachusetts

She wouldn't be happy if we hung her with a new rope.
Mrs. Mary J. Adkins, Leitchfield, Kentucky

He's as happy as a woodpecker in a 100-acre deadening.
*[A deadening is a place in a lake with dead trees sticking
out of the water]*

Well, I'm feeling as fine as snuff.

I'm cooking on a front burner today. *[Feeling good]*

I feel fat and sassy, thank you.

That baby reminds me of a tree full of young owls. *[When
baby is amused]*

He lost his possum and he has to do his own grinning.

In order to survive, you have to be happier than if you
were in your right mind.

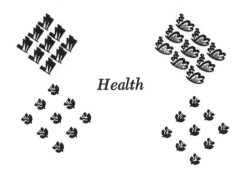

Health

FAIR TO MIDDLIN'

I've got a heart as sound as a cabbage.

I'm not doin' half that bad at all.

How in the health are you?

I ate lots of sow belly with the buttons on. *[Feeling fit]*
Ruth Marlels, Renton, Washington

Don't you feel too pretty bad today?
Martha Madsen, Milwaukee, Wisconsin

I'm like a dead horse—I can't kick.

I'm feelin' fair to middlin'.

93

A PERFECT GENTLEMAN IS ONE WHO CAN DRIVE A VERY SMALL CAR WITH TWO GIRLS IN THE FRONT SEAT AND CHANGE GEARS WITHOUT GETTING HIS FACE SLAPPED.

SAM LEVENSON

One of my favorite comedians and humorists is Sam Levenson. He has spent a lifetime collecting sayings and phrases from people in every walk of life. The first person I called before starting this book was Sam, and I asked him for a few of his favorites, along with an idea or two on how these catch phrases got started. Sam told me this:

There's only one human life and there are not too many variations. There are linguistic variations because each one of us was raised in a different minor culture. The major culture is humanity, and I have found that some of the sayings, proverbialisms, catch phrases, metaphors, similes and slang have become part of the language of the people.

Once in a while someone comes up with a line that's fresh and startling. There are expressions that start within a family around a certain situation, and then spread to the world outside.

For example: "It's like Uncle Sam and the cannon." Now, who knows Uncle Sam? Nobody else, but to the family it means something. Let's build on this premise.

95

We had an Uncle Sam who sent a picture from the first World War. It shows him standing there with a helmet, ribbons, and a cannon. Now, here's the punch line—the next day, after the picture was taken, he was rejected by the draft board. You never saw such a soldier-hero in your life—they never even took him in the service.

So, anytime anyone did anything prematurely, the family said, "Remember Uncle Sam and the cannon," and it became a phrase.

Then there's restaurant lingo. When waiters call in orders, they might say: "Adam 'n' Eve on a raft" (two poached eggs on toast). A tossed salad is "Shake up the garbage can." "One mixed marriage" is cream cheese and lox on Irish bread. That's colorful language.

Now, people like my father, who didn't even speak English, have languages all their own. He used to create phrases so he could be understood.

"What's the matter?" is English, but my father would say "Vatsumatter?" I didn't realize that *vatsumatter* meant something different to my father than it meant to me. One day he came home, and there must have been an accident on the corner, because he came up and said, "Boy, did I see a vatsumatter!" So I asked myself what this meant. How did it add up? It seems that when he was witnessing this, people on the corner were all saying, "Vatsumatter, vatsumatter, vatsumatter!" So naturally he thought that it had to be a vatsumatter. That's how a phrase gets its start. We still say, "Why make such a vasumatter out of it?" in our family.

Or, how about if someone said, "Answer the hoozit?" Before the phone, if you lived in a tenement house, downstairs over the mailbox there was a little speaker and that carried all the way upstairs to the kitchen. So, when the buzzer rang, my mother would say, "Answer the hoozit." We would say, "Hoozit?" instead of "Who is it?" That's how a phrase or saying gets started.

In my new book, *You Don't Have to Be in Who's Who to Be in What's What,* I explore many of our verbal gems, but here are a few that have never been published, for *Country Talk:*

He's the kind of a fellow who will pat you on your back in front of your face and cut your throat behind your back.

I'll believe in capital punishment as long as it ain't too severe.

Gentlemen, for your information, I'd like to ask a question. *[At a budget hearing]*

The woman ran so fast, she couldn't catch her breast.

On returning from the doctor's office, he told his wife that he had too much castor oil in his blood. *[Cholesterol]*

The next time I take you anywhere, I'm going to leave you home! *[My father said this to me]*

Where can I find the bathroom stationery? *[Woman in supermarket]*

I've been in bed with my doctor for two weeks and it hasn't done me no good.

During the American Revolution, the crowned heads of Europe were trembling in their shoes.

He looks like he's been sorting wildcats. *[Of a prize-fighter]*

The great advantage to a democracy is that only one of these guys can get elected.

Give your child a spanking. If you don't know why, he does.

You're never too old to learn something stupid.

Liars

YOU'RE ALL WET!

He's so crooked he could hide behind a corkscrew.

You've got a good line, only the clothespin fell off.

You're all wet. [Response to a fishy story]

If you think fishermen are the biggest liars in the world, ask a jogger how far he runs in the morning.
Mrs. M. E. Karl, Wauskesha, Wisconsin

I think I hear ducks quacking in York State. [To teller of tall tales]

He's as shifty as a barrelful of snakes.

He talks out of both sides of his face.

You look like a sheep-killing dog. [To imply guilt]

You lie like a tombstone.

He lies like a used car salesman.

That fellow is so crooked he has to screw his pants off.

Trashy people would lie and steal just like any respectable congressman today.

He's as bilingual as a politician.
Clifton Brame, San Antonio, Texas

101

Loose Morals

LOOSE
AS A GOOSE

She's as busy as her bed on payday night.

Her paw would turn her picture to the wall.

She's as loose as a goose.

Are you looking for a little poontang? [*Want to mess around?*]

She's trashy poor and no 'count.

She threw her hat over the windmill. [*Behaved indiscreetly*]

You're as loose as a bucket of soot.

She's wilder than a peach orchard boar.
                                    Richard Duncan, Dallas, Texas

Her baby is descended from the long line she listened to.

WHEN YOU DROP A KNIFE, SOMEONE'S THINKING ABOUT YOU. WHEN YOU DROP A FORK, YOU'RE GOING TO HAVE COMPANY.

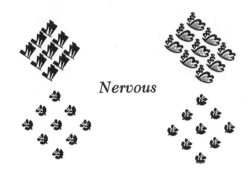

Nervous

AT THE END
OF THE ROPE

I'm so nervous, I feel like biting nails.
Mabel P. Smith, Catskill, New York

I got the wigglies.

I'm more nervous than the fleas on a skinny dog's belly.

He's sweating like an "Aggie" writing a business letter.

He's like a pea in a hot skillet, he's so nervous.

He's so nervous, he's sitting on the anxious seat.

He's as calm as a Texas cyclone.

She's as nervous as an old maid in an asparagus patch.
Mrs. John Candrilli, Troy, New York

She's so nervous, she's like a frog out on the highway with his hopper busted.

She's as jumpy as a cricket on a hot stove.

She's as restless as a hen on a hot griddle.

He's as nervous as a pregnant jenny in a traffic jam.

She's as nervous as a whore in church.

He's as nervous as a porcupine in a balloon factory.

I'm as nervous as a fly in a gluepot.

He's as nervous as a cat on a hot tin roof, trying to cover up his doo-doo.

He's got a burr under his saddle.

I don't know whether to shit or go blind.

I'm at my wits' end.

I'm so upset, I'm at the end of my rope.

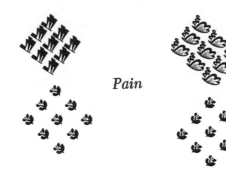

Pain

HURTIN'
FOR CERTAIN

111

I've got the whistlebelly thumps and the back door trots.

I have a head like a five-shilling pot. [*Hangover*]

I feel pretty good—except I have a skull cramp. [*Head-ache*]

I feel as sore as a boil.

I've got the green apple nasties.

It hurts right smart.

He's squawkin' like a hen layin' a square egg.
H. D. Eckard, Louisville, Kentucky

He gives me a pain I can't locate.

113

It's better to pass gas and bear the shame than not to pass gas and bear the pain.

I gotta make my bladder gladder, 'cause I'm hurtin' for certain.

I feel like an old window—all full of panes.

I got the epizootus. *[Feeling vaguely sick]*

Bill sure does look like death warmed over.

I'm sick in bed on two chairs.

I'm fit as a fiddle that's out of tune.

He's got one foot in the grave and the other one on a banana peel.

He looks as though one more clean shirt would do him in.
                                        Margaret Hart, Rome, New York

MAN WHO CROSSES BRIDGE BEFORE HE GETS TO IT PAYS TOLL TWICE.
                        Allan Dale, WOAI, San Antonio, Texas

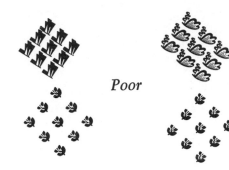

Poor

POOR AS
A CHURCHMOUSE

He saves at the spigot and lets it run out the bunghole.

He's so poor, if Cadillacs were selling for five dollars, he couldn't honk the horn on a Model T.

He's on the ragged edge. *[Penniless]*

He's too poor to paint and too proud to whitewash.

Their ground is so poor that they couldn't afford to raise a row with a pitchfork.

His shoes are so thin he could stand on a dime and tell you if it was heads or tails.

He's turning handsprings for hot dogs. *[Singing for his supper]*

117

He's so poor he couldn't buy hay for a nightmare.

Poor people have poor ways.

They're so poor they're eating bread dipped in fried water.

Some people are so poor that even the poor people call them poor.

I'm not broke, but badly bent.

I'm so broke I can't even pay attention.

We were so poor we kept the wolf too scared to stop at the door.

He's poor as a rail.

We're so poor this week we're going to have to put the mirror on the table and eat on our good looks.
Janet C. Cabelick, Milwaukee, Wisconsin

I wish I had been born rich instead of so goodlooking.

I'm so poor I'd have to sit on a sack of fertilizer to raise an umbrella.

Money is the root of all evil, and I would like to be evil for just one day.

Pretty

PRETTY
AS A PICTURE

She's as pretty as a baldfaced heifer.

She's as pretty as a speckled pup under a red wagon.

I'd rather watch her walk than eat fried chicken.

She looks gooder than a blue ribbon bull.

You have just captured my heart and about three other organs.

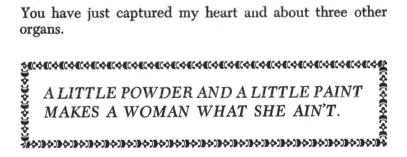

A LITTLE POWDER AND A LITTLE PAINT MAKES A WOMAN WHAT SHE AIN'T.

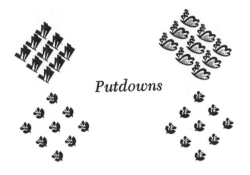

Putdowns

COTTON-PICKIN' SO-AND-SO

You're not worth a milk bucket under a bull.

Some people get paid to sing, but you ought to be horse-whipped.

What did you do with the money your mother give you for singing lessons? *[To someone singing off-key]*

You're about as safe as a rooster in the barnyard and the preacher's coming to dinner.

You don't need that anymore than a tomcat needs a marriage license.

You're so low you'd have to look up to see Hell.

You're so low I couldn't put a rug under you.

You are just a pimple on the face of history.
Robert D. Ingis, Hillsdale, New York

You've got a head harder than a nine-pound bag of jaw-breakers.

Stan Robbins, Santa Clara, California

You're so low you could play handball against the curb.

That will last as long as a paper shirt in a bear fight.

You're as graceful as an elephant on roller skates.

Esther Meyer, Milwaukee, Wisconsin

He's as nimble as a cow in a cage.

You may think you are the only pebble on the beach, but they have a little rock in Arkansas.

You haven't the chance of a one-legged man at an ass-kicking contest.

Jerry Hudson, Beaumont, Texas

You are as handy as a wee teapot without a spout.

Margaret North, Herkimer, New York

You cotton-pickin', chicken-pluckin' so-and-so!

Don't change. I want to forget you as you are.

You are going to break your arm patting yourself on the back.

Don't crow so loud, rooster, you might lay an egg.

You sound like a dying calf in a thunderstorm.

Mr. and Mrs. Wayne Brandon, Rogers, Arkansas

You smell like you want to be left alone.

Your room smells like a monkey cage on the Fourth of July.

There are two people I don't like and you are both of them.

If bullshit was music, you'd have a brass band.

You have enough brass in your face to make a kettle.

He's sour enough to curdle milk.

It sounds like you have a mouthful of mush.

Anytime you happen to pass my house, I'd sure appreciate it.

Hang it in your ear and twist it twice.

Get off your high horse and come down to earth.

Don't be so high and mighty. Come off the roof.

You make me pually tiahd. *[Purely tired]*

Go around the block three times and come back twice.

You've got a head full of cheese.

You couldn't knock a hole in the wind with a fistful of hammers.

He's no more good to me than a needle without an eye.
                              Matild Kuperberg, Miami, Florida

He wobbles like a drunken sailor with two left legs.

He's as in and out as a dog's hind leg. *[Undependable]*

He learned to swim in a tar rut.

127

He has to put a piece of meat in his hip pocket to get a dog to come to him.

He's so sorry he has to get up on a stump to kiss a snake's belly.

He sups up sorrow by the spoonful.

He's a mean old hound dog that wouldn't take the time to scratch his momma's fleas.

G. H. Brush, Dallas, Texas

He's mean enough to take his wife's egg money.

He's lower than a snake's belly in a wagon rut.

He lives so far out in the country that sunlight has to be piped to him every morning.

He lives so far in the boondocks that his idea of a seven-course dinner is a six-pack and a possum.

He's such a loser he bought a suit with two pairs of pants and burned a hole in the jacket.

He's like a blister. He don't show up until after the work is done.

He's so lazy, he wouldn't say "Sooey" if the hogs were eating him up.

He's like a snake without a pit to hiss in.

I'd like to buy him for what he's worth and sell him for what he thinks he's worth.

M. M. O'Dowd, Queen of Hog Creek, Tennessee

These scissors won't cut hot butter.

He bellows like a calf in a hailstorm.

That city slicker wouldn't know a bull from a cow if it didn't have a ring through its nose.

He has no more chance than a grasshopper in a chicken house.

He thinks he's hot snot, but he's just cold boogers.

He is so absentminded he sent his wife to the bank and kissed his money goodbye.

He's so conceited he keeps a mirror on the bathroom ceiling so he can watch himself gargle.

He's so weak he couldn't put a dent in a pound of hot butter.

That kid isn't spoiled. He always smells that way.

He would argue with a signpost.

He couldn't get a prostitute a date on a troop train.

He's so negative that when he goes into a room, it's like somebody leaving.

He's so contrary he can float upstream.
Martha Noble, Benson, Vermont

Looks are deceiving. He's not as normal as he appears.

He's so bad he'd steal the flowers from his grandmother's grave.

He acted in a clap-happy manner. *[Foolish]*

They call her radio station. Anyone can pick her up— especially at night.

She's so spoiled that salt wouldn't save her.

She has a tongue like a bellclapper.

She's all over him like a cheap suit.

She was bred in Kentucky, but she's just a crumb here.

She has more nerve than a toothache.

Mrs. Joan Nichols, Fort Erie, Ontario

She walks like an old hen with an egg broken inside of her.

I don't trust him as far as I can throw a piano.

I wouldn't send you a bale of hay if you were a donkey in a concrete pasture.

I wouldn't vote for him to tote feed to a bear.

Curtis Mitchell, Texas

Let's play horse. I'll play the front end, and you just be yourself.

I have a tie that isn't as loud as you.

She's itching for something she's not willing to scratch for.

She's the biggest agitator since the first washing machine.

Speed

GREASED LIGHTNIN'

I'll be there quicker than two shakes of a lamb's tail.

He's as fast as greased lightnin'.

Why, I could walk and lead a mule faster than that.

The faster I go, the behinder I get.

He's driving so fast he's trying to catch up with yesterday.

He's goin' like a bat out of hell.

He's driving like a blue-ass fly.
                              Lois Peck, Pompano Beach, Florida

Rattle your slats. [Get moving]

He's going hell-bent for election.

I had a mule so fast you had to tell him "whoa" before you told him "giddy up."

She sews with a hot needle and galloping thread.

I'm running as fast as my fat little legs will carry me.

He took off like a duck in a hailstorm.

That's faster than double-geared lightning.

He ran faster than a scalded cat.

He took off like a ruptured duck.

133

I can do that quicker than a minnow can swim a dipper.

He got there faster'n you could pluck a chicken.

He's quick like a bunny.

He's going like a house on fire.

He's going as fast as a sneeze through a mitten.
                                    Jill Coitrone, Augusta, Maine

As quick as a gnat's eye.
                                Raymond Henkle, Seattle, Washington

He went down the road like a pay train passing a tramp.

He can stop on a dime and give you nine cents change.

He moves as slow as a snail's gallop.

You are as slow as Christmas.

He's as slow as the seven-year itch.

He's so slow he has to speed up to stop.

It's as slow as suckin' buttermilk through a straw.

You're so slow you couldn't catch a cold.

It's as slow as cold molasses creeping uphill in January.

Slower than a turtle in a barrel of molasses.

THE BEST YEAR-ROUND TEMPERATURE IS A WARM HEART AND A COOL HEAD.

Stupidity

DUMB
AS A DOORKNOB

If brains were leather, he wouldn't have enough to saddle a flea.

He couldn't hit the floor if he fell out of bed.

Don't confuse me with facts. My mind's made up.

I'm so mixed up I don't know whether to wind my hair or scratch my watch.

You're just like a dog chasing a car. If you caught a girl, you wouldn't know what to do with her.

He doesn't know whether he's afoot or ahossback.

He's so stupid he doesn't know if he's washing or hanging out.

He's as nutty as a peach orchard borer.

He has a hole in his screen door.

He's a silly-ass cadet.

He couldn't track an elephant in four feet of snow.

He carries his brains in his back pocket.

You are a squirrel's idea of Utopia—nuts.

That ol' boy is just natural sorry.

James Osborne, Texas

He's like talking to a bedpost.

If you put his brains in a hummingbird's head, it would fly backwards.

Julie Stanford, Austin, Texas

Don't just stand there like an ox on a hill.

He's as dumb as a rubbin' post.

All asses do not go on four feet.

You remind me of yesterday's coffee—a little weak in the bean.

His head is as empty as last year's bird's nest.

He has the I.Q. of a watermelon.

He doesn't have his oars in the water.

If you had a brain, it would be lonely.

Hang crepe on your nose, your brains are dead.

He talks like a book with no pages in it.

She's dumber than a doorknob.

He's dumb enough to be twins.

He doesn't have all his shirts, which is worse than not having all his buttons.

He's narrow between the eyes, like a perch.

He doesn't know beans from buttons.

Mrs. P. R. Howard, Freehold, New Jersey

He's so stupid he thinks the Mexican border pays rent.

She'd have to study hard to be a half-wit.

He has no more idea than a bat-eyed spook.

He doesn't know "sic 'em" from "come here."

He ain't got the sense that God gave little apples.

She's pretty fly. *[Scatterbrained]*

He's got an unfinished attic. *[Not too bright]*

Anna Ford, Dorchester, Massachusetts

He's three bricks shy of a full load.

He doesn't know whether it's pancake Tuesday or half-past breakfast.

He couldn't find his rear end if it was on fire.

She doesn't know beans from bullfrogs.

He's a little slow on the draw.

He's twelve cookies short of a dozen.

He's so stupid he thought manual labor was a Mexican.

He was born ignorant and he's been losing ground ever since.

He has a head like a mallet.

She's so slow that whenever the bell rings on her typewriter she thinks it's time for coffee break.

He can't ride a horse and chew tobacco at the same time.

His bread ain't baked.

If brains were ink, you couldn't dot an "i."

You were under the table when they passed out the brains.

When they were passing out brains, he thought they said "trains" and got out of the way.

If you yelled in his ears, you'd probably hear an echo.

He's not tightly wrapped.

She's so dumb, it takes her an hour to make minute rice.

He's three pickles short of a barrel.

He's so dumb he couldn't find his own butt with both hands, a compass and a flashlight.

He doesn't have brains enough to pound sand down a rat hole.

He didn't come to town on the first load of pumpkins.
                        Maxine Line, Tulsa, Oklahoma

He's too dumb to pour piss out of a boot with instructions on the heel.

                        Paul Busby, New York City

You Talk
Too Much

BEATING YOUR GUMS

The way you are shooting off your mouth, you must have
had bullets for breakfast.
                    Gilbert Clevenger, Los Gatos, California

He has a mouth as big as a ten-gallon bucket.

Your mouth will keep you out of heaven.

Stop beating your gums to death.

He talks too fast and listens too slow and always winds
up with his foot in his mouth.

He could talk a dog's hind legs off.

I hear you clucking, but I can't find your nest.

She speaks 140 words a minute, with gusts of up to 180.

Why don't you freeze your teeth and give your tongue a sleighride?

You talk like a sausage with the end bit off.
John Bitney, Oak Creek, Wisconsin

Her tongue wags at both ends.

She could talk the legs off a chair.

He is transmitting when he should be receiving.

He could talk the ears off a brass monkey.

His tongue is tied in the middle and loose at both ends.

Listen, this is my duck—let me milk it. *[To someone butting in]*

I think you'd better leave because you've got diarrhea of the oral cavity.

He's such a talker, he blowed in on his own wind.

He could talk a cow out of her calf.

His jaw was exercised a-plenty, puttin' in a big crop of words.

They ought to hire him to keep the windmill goin'.

He could talk a pump into believing it's a windmill.

He could talk the hide off a cow.

He talked till his tongue hung out like a cow rope.

His tongue is plumb frolicsome.

There he goes with that chin music again.

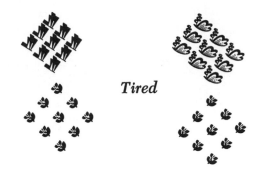

Tired

TUCKERED OUT

I feel like a bar of soap after a Saturday night bath.

He looks like a piece of chewed twine.

I was born tired and suffered a relapse.

I'm near about past goin'.

I'm as tired as a little by golly.

I'm going to have a kink. *[Fisherman term for snooze]*

I get up so early that I meet myself going to bed.

He gets up so early in the morning he has to pry up the sun with a crowbar.

I have the big-eye. *[Can't get to sleep]*

I'm powerful tired. Right now I feel like I've got one wheel down and my axle draggin'.

You look like a weasel peeking through a sieve.
                              Elna Fisk, North Hoosick, New York

I was called, couldn't go; went anyway and weren't wanted. *[Tired]*

147

Ugly

UGLY AS
A MUD FENCE

You were so ugly when you were born the doctor slapped your mother.

Your ears are so big you look like a taxi with the doors open.

You're so ugly only a mother could love you—on payday.

If anyone kidnaps you, they'll drop you off near the first lamp post.

You look like you were sent for and couldn't come.

You look like a million dollars—all green and wrinkled.

Your eyes are like two boiled onions in a cellar wall.

Your eyes look like rat droppings in a snowbank.

Your teeth are like the stars—they come out night.

You have friendly eyes—they always look at each other.

Your teeth are like pearls—they're so scarce.

He's so ugly, when he looks in the mirror, his reflection throws up.

He looks like he's been drawn through a knothole backwards.

His feet are so large he gets his shoes from a blacksmith.

He's so bowlegged he couldn't stop a pig at the gate.

He's so bald he parts his hair with a towel.

She has tongue enough for ten rows of teeth.

Her hair has been dyed so many times that the dandruff is Technicolored.

She looks like a professional blind date.

She's as homely as a screen door in a submarine.

She's so bucktoothed she could eat corn through a picket fence.

She's so ugly she has to sneak up on a glass of water.

She's as homely as a picket fence.

She's as ugly as home-made sin.

She's as ugly as a mud fence.

This gal is so ugly she has to slap her feet to make them go to bed with her.

She's so ugly her mother takes her everywhere she goes so she doesn't have to kiss her goodbye.

She's so ugly her face looks like it wore out four bodies.

She has so many freckles she looks like she swallowed a dollar and broke out in pennies.

She's so ugly the tide wouldn't take her out.

She looks like she's been chewed up, spit out, and stepped on.

She's as ugly as forty miles of bad road.

She looks like she's been whupped with an ugly stick.

She can't help being ugly, but she could stay home.

Beauty is skin deep, but ugly goes clear to the bone.

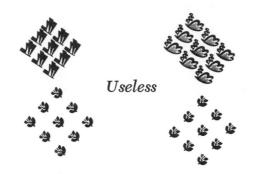

Useless

TITS ON
A BOAR HOG

155

It's useless to ask him to behave like a human being. He doesn't do imitations.

He needs that like a fish needs a bicycle.

I need that as much as a sow needs a sidesaddle.

She's as useless as a tit on a boar hog, and you can't get any more useless than that.

She's as useless as an umbrella to a duck.

It's not worth the spit to wet a postage stamp.
Lynn Craig, W. Allis, Wisconsin

He has as much use for that as a hog with a Sunday hanky.
Rusty Sharp, N. Vernon, Indiana

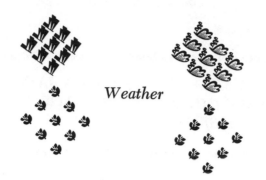

Weather

HOT AS BLAZES

A FAMILY UNIT IS LIKE A BANK. IF YOU TAKE OUT MORE THAN YOU PUT IN, IT GOES BROKE.

It's hotter than a hen layin' eggs in a woolen basket.

It's hotter than burning stump.

It's hotter than a desert rat's armpit.
Norman Cooney, Palmer, Ohio

It's hotter in here than a June bride's featherbed.

It's as hot as a billygoat in a pepper patch.

It's as hot as a fiddler's pup.

It's hotter than a depot stove.

It's hotter than a French kissed fox in a forest fire.

It's too hot to trot.

It's so hot an egg could fry before it hits the ground.

It's hotter than honeymoon sheets.

It's as hot as a preacher at a singin'.

It's as hot as a $2.00 pistol.

It was so hot I saw a cat chase a dog and they were both walking.

It's hotter than the hind hubs of perdition.

I'm as hot as a little train.

It's hotter than a two-peckered billygoat.

It's so hot the hens are laying hardboiled eggs.

It's hotter than a preacher's knee.

It's as hot as a tater bug.

It's one light shirt and no suspenders weather.

I'm as hot as a firecracker, lit on both ends and poppin' in the middle.

Snow is angels shaking their bedding.

If it's coming a snow, I hope it's a good one, hub deep to a Ferris wheel.

It's as cold as flugers.

It's colder than a witch's tit in a cast-iron bra.
                    Julie Freeman, N. Hollywood, California

It's as cold as kraut.

It's as cold as a stepmother's kiss.

It's colder than a witch's kiss.
Dan Angst, Puyallup, Washington

It's as cold as snow in harvest.

It was so cold I saw a chicken cross the street with a capon.

It's as cold as a welldigger's behind in the Klondike.

There's nothing between Texas and the North Pole but a barbed wire fence.

It's colder than a cast-iron commode on the shady side of an iceberg.

It's jeezly cold. *[Very cold, Greenville, Maine]*

It's so cold out that the mercury dropped right out of the thermometer, went down seven clapboards onto a rake handle and froze.

It's so cold my drawers feel like they're made of cheesecloth.

It was so cold that a third-degree Mason dropped one degree.
Harold Zwetfel, San Antonio, Texas

It's cold enough to freeze the balls off a brass monkey.

It's colder than a freezer full of sheared sheep.

It's colder than an iceman's shoulder.
Ed Fisher, WBBG Radio, Cleveland, Ohio

Close your neck and shut the window—it's cold.
Charlotte Kimmel, North Lauderdale, Florida

It's gatherin' up a norther. *[Cold front coming]*

I'm as cold as a frog.

I'm drier than a pop corn fart.

It's drier than an unprimed water pump.
Michael Stewart, Garland, Texas

It's so dry I could spit cotton.

It looks like it's going to well up and rain.

Here comes a gullywasher.

It's as wet as a frosted frog.

It's raining puppydogs and pussycats.

It's raining pitchforks and little babies.

Looks like it's comin' a frog-strangler.

It's a sittin'-in rain.

We hain't had airy a rain the whole month.

It's been right smart dry.

It's been fixin' to fair off.

We have sandstorms so thick the dogs try to dig holes in the air.
Lubbock, Texas

The mildest winter I ever spent was a summer on Puget Sound.
Mark Twain

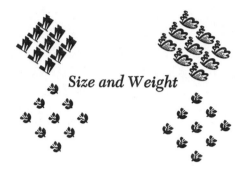

Size and Weight

KNEE-HIGH TO A DUCK

ANYONE WHO THINKS BY THE INCH AND TALKS BY THE YARD OUGHT TO BE MOVED BY THE FOOT.

He's as big as a bar of soap after washday.

These eggs are so big it won't take many of 'em to make a dozen.

Albert Lee Wilson, Frankfort, Kentucky

She's big enough to go bear-hunting with a stick.

That's bigger 'n Dallas.

I'd rather shake than rattle. *[Said by a plump woman]*

Everything you eat you wear well.

She's so fat, if she fell down, she'd rock herself to sleep before you could pick her up.

She's built like a wagon tongue—heavy where the pin goes in.

E. C. Hart, Minerva, Ohio

That ol' lard ass.

He's like a blind dog in a meathouse. *[Overweight man near food]*

From behind, she looks like two cabbage heads in a gunny sack.

From behind, she looks like two little hogs boxing in a gunny sack.

He's so skinny he has to wear skis in the shower to keep from going down the drain.

She's so skinny, if she turned sideways and stuck out her tongue, she'd look like a zipper.

It's as light as a fiddlestring.

You look like a bedbug tied in the middle. *[Tight belt]*
                                    Joyce Cosier, Massilon, Ohio

She's so skinny she ought to trade legs with a killdeer.

She looks like a gutted snowbird.

She's as slender in the middle as a cow in the waist.

She's so thin she could lie under a clothesline and not get sunburned.

She's so skinny she has to stand twice to make a shadow.

She's so skinny you could lose her in a wrinkle of the sheet.

She's as thin as a rake and twice as sexy.

This gal was so skinny you could feed her a little red soda pop and use her for a thermometer.

He's so skinny he looks straight up and down, like an outhouse door.
                                    Margaret North, Herkimer, New York

He's knee-high to a duck.

It's all cut up like a boarding house pie. *[Something divided into many pieces]*

Her kitchen isn't big enough to cuss a cat in without getting a mouthful of fuzz.

She's smaller than a gnat's whisker.
                                    Pat Crouse, Houston, Texas

Hello & Goodbye

I'M HUNGRY TO SEE YOU

THE HARDEST THING TO LEARN IN LIFE IS WHICH BRIDGE TO CROSS AND WHICH BRIDGE TO BURN.

HOSPITALITY IS THE FINE ART OF MAKING YOUR GUESTS WANT TO STAY, WITHOUT INTERFERING WITH THEIR DEPARTURE.

Come on over and we'll chaw the rag awhile.

Have a chair and sit down beside it. *[Texas wit to make guest Mary Alice O'Dowd, Queen of Hog Creek, feel welcome]*

Come and see us. We'll do so many nice things for you, you're bound to like some of them.

Arkansas

If ye shoot up the alley, I'll give you a shout.

May you be in heaven a half hour before the devil knows you're dead.

I'm getting hungry to see you.

I'll be there if nothing breaks or comes untwisted.

I'll see you when two Sundays come together.

Come then to get me over or call me yet.
Fran Tessler, Wauwatosa, Wisconsin

When you come to my house, whistle me out so my ma will know who I hang by.
Marianne Goran, Greendale, Wisconsin

May the wind at your back never be your own.

Come back when you can't stay as long.

Who looks at the time when good friends are here? Why, it's only 12:18 and a half.

Don't go away mad—just go away.
Mrs. W. Lambrecht, Milwaukee, Wisconsin

See ya next week, if the Lord is willing and the creek don't rise.

See ya round like a donut and long as a cruller.

I think we'll go to bed so you can leave. *[To late company]*

Buzz away like a bumblebee.

Make like a hockey player and get the puck out of here.

He was off like a jug handle. *[Left quickly]*

Plant the corn in the right place. *[What you say to others when you are leaving on trip]*

He's off like a dirty shirt.

Have a nice trip . . . see you next fall. *[To someone who has just tripped]*

Come good home. *[Arrive safely; Milwaukee]*

Go peddle your peanuts elsewhere.

He's as welcome as a skunk at a lawn party.

She's as welcome as the flowers in May.

He's as welcome as snow in winter.

He's as welcome as water on a leaking ship.

He's as welcome as water in your shoe.

Sit on the floor and hang off your feet.

Pull up a chair and sit a spell.

Howzit goin', y'all?

Why you no hello me when you know me so easy?
Ronald W. Norell, Milwaukee, Wisconsin

That road has so many curves you meet yourself coming
back.
Gloria Kolchmainen, Milwaukee, Wisconsin

He has his sittin' britches on. *[Of someone who stays too
long]*

He stays until the last dog is hung.

Country Phrases

SLAP
MY PAPPY

175

Your ox won't plow. *[Of anything not performing the function for which it was intended]*

It's like putting socks on a rooster.

It's like trying to catch a bag of flies.

You come so early—so late!

It's like throwing a saddle on a dead horse.

It's like finding a bird's nest on the ground. *[Unexpected good luck]*

I'm up the river without a paddle.

Eat, eat, old man's in the stove. *[My husband's dinner is in the stove]*

Go over yonder, while I ponder.

Broom off the sidewalk . . . the sidewalk's getting tick. *[Dirty]*

Thadd Hrymiewiecki, Milwaukee, Wisconsin

Fish, cut bait, or go ashore. *[Make up your mind]*

Rock him round the corner. *[Get out of here]*

Massachusetts

Spec o' ice'll fix it. *[Boston cure-all]*

Come July we start barning tobacco.

How's your mom'nem? *[Mom and them]*

I'm going sparking. *[To visit best boy/girl friend]*

Do whatever melts your butter. *[Whatever pleases you]*

I'm gonna put down the laundry. *[Do the wash]*
Peggy Hubsch, New Orleans, Louisiana

He's pulling a monkeyshine. *[Trick]*

Oh dear, bread and beer!

Go to bed, I'm tired. Put on your coat, I'm cold.
Nancy Crooks, Milwaukee, Wisconsin

Where's the groceries? *[When do we eat?]*

Throw a tub to the whale. *[Give in]*

He cleaned your plow. *[Had the last word]*

178

Grab that poke and go get some taters. *[Farmer to his son]*

Mrs. R. M. Pratt, Drumright, Oklahoma

Don't take any wooden nickels or swim any dry creeks.

Let it rest until the good is better and the better is best.

That's your possum and you can just wool it. *[Your problem]*

Pucker up and slip me a slobber.

If you go out and break both your legs, don't come running to me.

Now, wouldn't that blow your dress up? *[Something unusual happening]*

She's sittin' on the nest. *[She's pregnant]*

She's got one in the oven. *[Ditto]*

She swallowed a punkin seed. *[Ditto]*

Does a bear sleep in the woods? *[Of the obvious]*

Hurry up and get born! *[Wake up!]*

Can a cat lick his whiskers? *[Of the obvious]*

Doesn't that rip the rag right off the bush?

I'll jump on you with both feet. *[Reprimand]*

That's sad enough to bring a tear to a glass eye.

Lyndal Vanell, Garland, Texas

That will take the soles off your shoes. *[Surprise]*

179

That knife wouldn't cut butter if it was hot.

He got the wire brush treatment. *[After rough session with boss]*

He really got sandpapered. *[Had a rough time]*

She's an angel with horns, holding up a halo.

The boy's gone by with the cows and the snap's down. *[Lost opportunity]*

It's morning every night before I go to bed.

Did you swap slobbers? *[Did you kiss?]*

He's whistling past the graveyard. *[Scared]*

Bid 'em high and sleep in the street. *[Bad poker hand]*

You've got the saw by the wrong tree. *[Telling a story wrong]*

Slap my pappy. *[Gossip]*

They've got two lamps burning and no ships at sea. *[Wastefulness]*

We're not on borrowing terms.

They don't put their horses up together. *[Unfriendly]*

You betcha. *[You're welcome]*

The cake's all dough. *[Failure]*

I haven't seen Dick in some time, he's housed in.

I'm here to do God's work, whatever the hell it is.

Oh, twiddle twad. *[Don't believe it]*

Match me, big boy. *[Give me a light]*

He got kissed in the eye teeth. *[Hit in the mouth]*

That makes the cheese more binding. *[Agreement]*

Keep your bunnies in order. *[Don't go nuts]*

Honey and a bee ball, I can't see y'all. Y'all hid? *[Hide and seek chant]*

She's nursing on the hind tit.

Well, I'm goin' back to the bahn. *[Back home]*

He's gone back to the wagon yard. *[Home]*

That's dropping a rusty bucket down my well. *[Stepping on my toes]*

Stand aside and let the dog see the rabbit. *[Watching someone try to fix something]*

The pigs ran through it. *[Changed agreement]*

That accounts for the milk in the coconut. *[Explains the puzzle]*

The dog got no business in the cat fight. *[Stay out of other people's business]*

I'll give it back, railing for railing. *[Revenge]*

Pert near, but not plumb. *[Almost but not quite]*

He's juggin' and jawin'. *[Drinking and talking]*

Don't you mouth this to anyone.

I'm going to Maundy County. *[A need to get out of town]*

He's like an ole cow's tail, all behind. *[Behind in work]*

Go up on the roof and sweep the sun off it. *[Remedy for boredom]*

It was mighty thoughty. *[Thoughtful of you]*
Jorge Von Holstein, Richardson, Texas

You can't win for losing. *[Can't do anything right]*

He picked up his crumbs. *[Regained his health]*

Call me anything, but don't call me late for dinner.

I'm always a day late and a dollar short.

There's a fox in the house. *[Said of a young man visiting a family with daughters]*

I've got Indian underwear on. It keeps creeping up on me.

Go down and throw the horse over the fence some hay.
Pennsylvania Dutch

It's bare work and pore pay.

Hang a smile on your face and reminisce with me.
Mrs. Eleanor Grace, Wisconsin

Make with a smile for once. Some folks are wonderful nice.
Mrs. John Ebner, Louisville, Kentucky

What time is it on the wall hanging?
Anthony Cassata, Glendale, Wisconsin

Well, tickle my gizzard!

Throw father down the steps his hat.

Pennsylvania Dutch

If you feel froggy, leap! *[Jump for joy]*

Bushel of wheat and a bushel of rye. All not hid, holler "I." Here I come with both eyes open. *[Hide and seek chant]*

That's two buckets of possums. *[Two different situations]*

That's another basket of hangers. *[Ditto]*

Old Red's chewing his bits. *[The horse is anxious to go]*

They're so all fired up and full of git. *[A teacher of her kindergarten class]*

Pearl Weir, Louisville, Kentucky

Hes' got right smart A literature. *[He's educated]*

I'm as regular as a goose a-going barefoot.

You'll have to learn to butt with your own head. *[Take care of your own problems]*

Wait till I lock open the rear back door.

Violet Brosig, Milwaukee, Wisconsin

Did you button the door on the back house?

Kenneth Abbott, New York

Take the roof off the greenhouse, Mother, the corn's growin' higher.

Don't you try to crawfish out of that situation.

That'll cork your pistol. *[That will stop you]*

Who hit Nelly in the belly with the flounder?
                    Linda Leach, Melrose, Massachusetts

He's up a gump stump. *[A dead end]*
                    Robert Schaad, Mansfield, Ohio

A guilty fox hunts his own hole first.

If a frog had wings, its tail wouldn't touch the ground.

Quit hollering down the rain barrel. *[Don't waste your breath]*

What we got now is all, but when we get some more, we will give you any.
                    Milwaukee

If you are not careful, you'll get your tail in a crack.

It's easy to hold down the latch when nobody pulls the string.

Long may your big jib draw. *[Good luck—nautical]*

Give her the long main sheet. *[Go away and don't come back—nautical]*

RING TRUE

Don't be what you ain't.
Jes' be what you is.
If you is not what you am,
Then you am not what you is.
If you're just a little tadpole
Don't try to be a frog.
If you're just the tail,
Don't try to wag the dog.
You can always pass the plate,
If you can't exhort and preach.
If you're just a little pebble,
Don't try to be the beach.
Don't be what you ain't
Jes' be what you is,
For the man who plays it square,
Is a-goin' to get his.

                                —*Anon.*

I have three speeds when I dance: start, stumble and fall.

That puts butter on the bacon. *[An improvement]*

Hose him down with cracked ice! *[Hot damn!]*

He's been on the cow's side of the fence. *[In the other guy's shoes]*

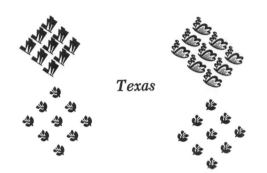

Texas

THE
LONE STAR STATE

Texas heat is where hell originated.

Don't spill the beans in Texas, just pass them.

Texans let it all hang out in Texas.

Why think it when you can say it in Texas?

These Texas roads are so crooked, I ran my battery down
blowing my horn at my own tail light.
                    Joseph T. Lee, San Antonio, Texas

The street plan of San Antonio was laid out by a drunk
Mexican on a blind mule.
                    Rick Barr, Universal City, Texas

He hit me like a Texas tornado.

You can believe what they say in Texas.

Y'all are at home in Texas.

Lucky me, Texas is my home.

Fort Worth is where the west begins.

HELL IN TEXAS

The devil in hell we're told was chained
And a thousand years he there remained.
He neither complained nor did he groan
But determined to start a hell of his own

Where he could torment the souls of men
Without being chained in an underground pen.
So he asked the Lord if he had on hand
Anything left when he made his land.

The Lord said, "Yes, I have plenty of land,
But I left it down on the Rio Grande.
The fact is, old boy, the stuff is real poor,
But you're welcome to it and plenty more."

So the devil went down to look at the truck
And said that if he took it as a gift he was stuck.
For after examining it carefully and well,
He concluded the place was too dry for a hell.

So in order to get it off his hand,
The Lord promised to water the land.
For he had some water, or rather some dregs—
Rather cathartic and smelled like bad eggs.

Hence the trade was closed and the deed was given
And the Lord went back to his home in heaven.
The devil said to himself, "I have all that is needed
To make a good Hell," and hence he succeeded.

He began to put thorns all over the trees
And mix up the sand with millions of fleas.
He scattered tarantulas along the roads;
Put thorns on cactus and horns on toads.

He lengthened the horns of the Texas steers
And put an addition to the rabbit's ears.
He put a little devil in the bronco steed
And poisoned the feet of the centipede.

The rattlesnake bites you, the scorpion stings,
The mosquito delights you with its buzzing wings.
Sand-burrs cause you to jig and dance
And those who sit down will have ants in their pants.

The devil said that throughout the land
He'd arrange to keep up the devil's own brand;
And all should be mavericks unless they bore
Marks and scratches, or bites by the score.

The heat in summer is one-hundred-and-ten
Too hot for the devil, too hot for the men.
Go see for yourself and you can tell
'Tis a hell of a place he has for hell.

—E. U. Cook, 1887
submitted by Florence Glazner
Dallas, Texas

191

TYPICAL TEXAS JARGON

"How y'all doin?" greeted Sara Jane.

"Well, look what the cat drug in!" exclaimed Pa. "Come in this house, girl! We're doin' tol'able well. How's things out your way?"

"Mighty fine, just hunky-dory. Can't stay, I've got to be goin' directly. You folks need ary a thing from town?"

"Why, lands, yes," said Ma. "Junior, hop down off'n that stool and fetch me my pocketbook. I need some sewing thread. Sister was so fidgety when I tried to hem up her dress that I got it all whomper-jawed. Now I'll have to take and do it all over again, but that skirt's right full, so I'll need a might more thread. Set a spell, Sara Jane, and rest your weary bones. It's hotter'n blue blazes out there. Land o' Goshen, that young'un can be faster'n greased lightnin' when it's time to play, but I'll be jiggered if he's not slower'n molasses when you send him on an errand!"

"Well, shoot a mile, ma'am," laughed Pa. "That there pocketbook of your'n is as big as a barrel and as heavy as lead. That boy'll be all tuckered out by the time he gets back!"

"Pshaw!" scoffed Ma. "Get off with you!"

"Here, Ma," sighed Junior. "That thing's so heavy it near 'bout tore my arm off! You oughta get one like Sary Jane's. It's flat as a flitter and light as a feather. Sary Jane, can I go with you? Please? Please, Pa, can I go?"

"Well, I swan, son, don't get all het up about it," drawled Pa. "It's a pretty fur piece to town and you're liable to fall out on the way. Now, no backtalk! You can talk till you are blue in the face, but that's just how the cow ate the cabbage."

"But, Pa!" whined Junior.

"Now, hesh up!" scolded Ma. "You can cry till the cows come home, but you'll just be whistlin' in the wind."

"Now, now, Junior, you just sit tight," said Sara Jane. "Town's not goin' nowhere. You can go with me another time. You've been my friend since you were knee-high to a grasshopper, and I'm not aimin' to forget you now."

So Sara Jane lit out for town, and everyone was happy as hogs in a wallow as they changed into their night-clothes and hit the hay.

—Bill and Sharon Booth
Mexia, Texas

Country
Wisdom

CAST YOUR BREAD
UPON THE WATER

If you want to be seen, stand up.
If you want to be heard, speak up.
If you want to be appreciated, shut up.

You can't no more do what you ain't been told than you
can go back to where you ain't come from.
Jennie and Bona Holbrook, Anchorage, Kentucky

One for a wish
Two for a kiss,
Three for a letter,
Four for something better,
Five for a tale of woe,
Six for a journey to go.

Any blind hog can find an acorn once in a while.

Luck is personal, not local.

No amount of planning will replace dumb luck.

Goodlooking women nowadays are as scarce as jug handles and hen's teeth.

As good as you are and as bad as I am, I'm as good as you are, as bad as I am.

Love is an itch of the heart you can't scratch.

Love doesn't make the world go round. It's what makes the ride worthwhile.

Love is like a circle—it has no end.

The game of love is dug with little digs.

A woman's love is like the morning dew. It's just as apt to fall upon a horse turd as it is upon a rose.

She's as cold as the beer that's brewed right here. If you don't believe it, whisper in her ear.

Dear, dear, bread and beer. If I were rich I wouldn't be here.
Angelina Conte, Revere, Massachusetts

Hens sit and lay and people sit and lie.

There are some people walking around dead and don't know enough to lie down.

Only asses make passes at lasses that wear glasses.

Apple pie without cheese is like a kiss without a squeeze.

Don't start chopping till you've treed the coon.

If you fool with the bull, you get the horn.

They don't send donkeys to school because no one likes a smart ass.
Dona Mileski, Kent, Ohio

The best form of taxation is that which will be paid by someone else.

Don't plant onions next to potatoes as the potatoes will cry their eyes out. *[Farmer's advice]*

He didn't mind the crackers in bed. It's when he came home and found the crumb in the closet.

Words are the fingers that mold the mind of man.

A squeaking wheel gets the grease but a quacking duck gets shot.

There is nothing more distant than a distant relative with money.

Home is the place we're treated the best and grumble the most.

It's not the size of the dog in the fight. It's the size of the fight in the dog.

Laurence Johnston, Corpus Christi, Texas

You don't live longer in the country. It just seems that way.

Hold your chin up high, but keep your nose at a friendly level.

There's no tree but bears some fruit. *[Goodness in everyone]*

Hell is God giving you what you thought you wanted.

A narrowminded person is no wider between the eyes than a case knife.

A push in the bush is worth two in the hand.

Little strokes fell great oaks.

A single line may have two hooks.
Ray Mickers, Louisville, Kentucky

Don't let the grass grow between your toes.

Experience is the best teacher, but the most expensive.

He who sits on a red hot stove shall rise again.

We get too soon old and too late smart.

Put your brain in gear before you put your mouth in motion.

Behind every white knight there's a set of dirty underwear.
Cheryl Fisher, Wisconsin

He who is always up in the air isn't necessarily an angel.
Alice E. Grohall

If your daughter wants to drive, don't stand in her way.
Ruth D. Ringe

The fool wanders and the wise man travels.

If you sing before breakfast, you'll cry before noon.

If you would enjoy fruit, pluck not the flower.

A wasteful wife can throw more out the window with a spoon than her husband can shovel in through the door.

The load is much lighter with more mules carrying it.

The wise man carries an umbrella when the sun shines— any fool knows enough to take it when it rains.
Lillian M. Gary

Reality is for people that can't handle drugs.

Work is the yeast that raises the dough.

A very strong man can move anything loose on one end.

No one flies so high but what they light on a cow dab.

A class reunion is where you get together to see who is falling apart.

It wasn't the apple on the tree that caused the trouble. It was the pair on the ground.

Whistling girls and crowing hens often come to no good ends.

Lorraine Harmon, Waukesha, Wisconsin

It's better to keep your mouth shut and seem a fool than open it and remove all doubt.

Those who travel with the owls at night can't fly with the eagles in the morning.

Kind words butter no parsnips.

Some people can't be jealous without showing it.

Martha Noble, Benson, Vermont

With the high cost of living, even the elephants are tired of working for peanuts.

That's life. If it isn't chickens, it's feathers.

He that would have the fruit must climb the tree.

Gum-chewing students and cud-chewing cows. There is a difference, you must allow. The intelligent look on the face of the cow.

To approach something straightforward is to take the bull by the tail and look the matter squarely in the face.

Get up, get up you lazy sinner. We need the sheet for a tablecloth and it's almost time for dinner.

Wait a fair wind, and you'll get one.

When someone sings his own praises, he always gets the tune too high.

The only mark some people make in this world is on somebody's fender.

Right's right and right don't wrong nobody.

An orchid is a weed in a cornfield.
The Baileys, Lynn, Massachusetts

What goes around comes around.

You shouldn't be so busy chopping wood that you forget to sharpen your axe.

Nothing has more lives than an error that you refuse to correct.

The proper pitch for some guitars is out the window.

Gossips get caught in their own mouthtraps.

If you invite trouble, don't complain if it accepts.
Peg Doersam, Springfield, Massachusetts

A wise man seldom changes his mind. A fool never does.

He only brushed when too wet to plow. He eats lots of mush 'cause he's gummin' it now.

They look so much together, when they're apart you can't tell the two of them from both. *[Identical twins]*
Milwaukee

Kissin' wears out. Cookin' don't.
Pennsylvania Dutch

Red up the room, outen the light, button don't make (bell doesn't ring).
Pennsylvania Dutch

A big barn and a plump wife, and a man is fixed off good for life.
Pennsylvania Dutch

When the sun is in the east, lazy people work the least. When the sun is in the west, lazy people work the best.

Happy is the home that welcomes a friend.

Happiness is found in little things.

Happiness is the reflection of a smile.

The easiest tasks are those done with love.

Always take the time to say what's in your heart.

The coldest days can produce the warmest smiles.
Mrs. Charlotte Rubaszek, Middle Grove, New York

Love is the nicest gift of all.

The happiest times are those shared with friends.

A guest in the house is God in the home.

A noisy cow gives little milk.

Hope keeps love alive.

He is rich who owns nothing.

A good appetite needs no sauce.

Hunger will lead the fox out of the forest.

The wiser the eggs, the wiser the chicken.

Without work there is no bread.

He who gives freely gives twice.

All times are good, when one is old.

The rabbits may hide in the forest, but a fox can always find them.

Country Words

BOONDOGGLE

As you've noticed, many of the words in Country Talk appear to have been made up, dug up, or spit up by some ol' boy who nearly graduated elementary school or some ol' codger in the sticks. The following are some words and terms and their definitions.

Aggervate　To annoy

Aggervation　If you can't figger this'n out, you jest ain't read the above.

Ayeh, Eyah, Ayuh　Yes (Maine)

Balky　A wino (Connecticut)

Belly bump　Riding a sled downhill flat on stomach

Bignet　French-style doughnut (New Orleans)

Binder　Rubber band (Minnesota)

Blinky　When milk gets old and sour but not yet clabbered (spoiled)

Bluestocking　A woman who will remain a spinster as long as there are sensible men on earth

Bobbing　Eel fishing

Boiled dinner　Heated argument (New England)

Boondoggle　Doing something rather badly that is hardly worth doing at all.

Boston cooler　Cantaloupe with ice cream (Pennsylvania); a tall glass of root beer with vanilla ice cream (Cleveland)

Briarpatch child   Born out of wedlock

Bucks   Money

Bought his thumb   Cheating (like the storekeeper who puts his thumb on the scale)

Cape Codder   Cranberry juice and vodka (New England)

Car boots   Tires

Car shoes   Brakes

Car bonnet   Hood of car

Chips   French fries (Canada, England)

Church stick   Light staff with rabbit foot on one end and a fox tail on the other, used to tickle anyone who had fallen asleep in church

Cider, store   Strained, boiled, and pasteurized cider

Cider, rotten apple   Cider from the squeezings of apples shoveled from the truck

Cider, russet   Cider made carefully from quality apples

Cider, hard   Vinegar or intoxicating drink

Clothes press   Closet (Pennsylvania Dutch)

Cock horse   An additional horse for getting heavy load up the hill.

Cocksure   Overconfident

Cold cellar   A room in the cellar of an old house for storage of food. (Also, root cellar)

(◄◄◄◄◄◄◄◄◄◄◄◄◄◄◄◄◄

College ice   Vanilla ice cream with chocolate sauce

A coon's age   A long time

Colorado Kool-Aid   Coor's beer

Copper   Old-time name for a penny

Corker   Remarkable person or thing

Cootie   A louse

Corke ball   Baseball (St. Louis)

Country bumpkin   Person from the country

Cowcumber   Cucumber (North Carolina)

Crank up the Car   Start the car (South Carolina)

Craw thumpers   Natives of Maryland

Cunnin'   Cute

Cat's pajamas   Very good. ("He's the cat's pajamas.")

Damn   Tre-damn-endous; fan-damn-tastic; incredi-damn-ble; hot damn; shoot-a-damn

Dinglefuzzie   What's-his-name

Dinner   Midday meal (North Carolina and elsewhere)

Dog fancier   Veterinarian

Dotlin   Small child

Double-dyed   Excellent quality

Duckins   Overalls

Duffer   Awkward fool

Dunnit: Ain't dunnit   It ain't so
       Is dunnit   It is so

Elastic   Rubber bands (New England)

Epizootic   Influenza afflicting horses in Boston, 1872

Eye-opener   Hooch, or straight whiskey

Fallen off   Lost weight

Fleshened up   Gained weight

Fetch or fotch   To bring

Fivey   Five-and-ten-cent store

Fixin'   Getting ready to do something

Flivver   A small, cheap car, usually old.

Fuddy duddy   Fussy person

Foose   Foam (on beer)

Footy McGander   Clumsy person

Footstove   Small square tin box filled with coals, taken to church to keep the feet warm.

Foozle   Work hurriedly and badly

Frog skins   Money

Frog-strangler   Heavy rain

Geedunk   Ice cream (Navy)

Giggle soup   Alcoholic beverage (North Carolina)

Glassie   Large marble made of glass

Godfrey mighty   An exclamation (Maine)

Greasy luck   Good luck

Ground hackey   Chipmunk (Pennsylvania)

Greengrocer   Vegetable market

Gumband   Rubber band (Pennsylvania Dutch)

Gunny sack   Gypsy word for bag or Italian petticoat

Half and half on rye   Boiled ham and swiss cheese
    (Pennsylvania)

Hand tub   Hand-operated fire engine

Hash: Red-flanned   With beets
    White-flanned   Without beets

Hatching jacket   Maternity blouse

Hayseed   Country bumpkin

A heapa folks   More folks than you can shake a stick at

Hey/hey, y'all   Hello

High-water pants   Pants that are too short

Hippen   Diaper (Tennessee)

Hitherwhich   Therefore

Hoedown   Squaredance

≪◆≪◆≪◆≪◆≪◆≪◆≪◆≪◆≪◆≪◆≪◆≪◆

Hogwallers   Mud holes

Hoity-toity   Putting on airs

Honeyfogle   To cheat by cajolery

Horning   Serenading newlyweds

Hot ticket   Fast girl

Huckleberry grunt   Cape Cod dessert

Humdinger   Something remarkable

Humpty schumpf   Good grief (Wisconsin)

Husher   Crocheted piece placed between a chamber pot and its lid to muffle the clang during the night.

Hysterical marker   Historical marker (Texas)

Irish turkey   Corned beef and cabbage

Jeans   Dungareens; dungarees; Wranglers; Levi's; dungies; blue jeans

Jimmies   Sprinkles on ice cream cones (Massachusetts)

Journey-proud   Enthusiastic about a trip

Juberous   Dubious (Texas)

Jularker   Boyfriend (North Carolina)

Kiver   Blanket (North Carolina)

Kopesetic   Everything is fine

Lay away   To bury a person

Lallygag   To flirt (1880)

Larrupin truck   Good food (Texas)

Later   Goodbye (Maine)

Liar's bench   Bench in front of a country store

Listers, the   Board of Assessors (New York)

Looseners   Prunes (1920)

Lost bread   French toast sprinkled with powdered sugar (New Orleans)

Machine   Car

Mess   Enough fish or vegetables for a meal (North Carolina)

Mess of sallet   Meal of greens (Tennessee)

Milkshake   Frappe (Boston); cabinet (Rhode Island); malted (New York); fribble; awful, awful; Frost.

Nary   None

Obfusticated   Bewildered (Utah)

Okie-dokie   OK

Panne meat   Breaded veal cutlet, browned with onions (New Orleans)

Parlor stove   Small woodburning stove in front room

Parson's nose   The part of the bird that went over the fence last

Pert neart   Very similar

Piddle-diddle   Procrastinate (North Carolina)

Pindling   Small and undernourished

Pizen   Poison (North Carolina)

Pizzlesprung   Pooped (Kentucky)

A *play pretty*   Toy (Mobile, Alabama)

Poke   Bag

Police cars   Prowl car (Los Angeles); black and white unit; paddywagon; black Maria; cruiser.

Porch   Stoop; veranda; piazza; gallery.

Pore   Poor

Privy   Outhouse; backhouse

Puckersnatch   Poor job of sewing

Raunchy   Mean and tough; also slovenly, smutty

Receipt   Recipe

Record player   Gramophone; Victrola; phonograph; hi-fi; stereo

Redney-buck   Redhead

Right much   Considerable amount (North Carolina)

Righten up   Tidy up a room (Maine)

Rotary   Traffic circle; battleground; neutral ground (New Orleans); dummy (Connecticut); circle (New Jersey)

Ruddle   Attic

Sack   Bag

Salt City savage   A citizen of Grand Saline, Texas. A loathsome being.

Sandwiches   Sub-spucky (Boston); grinder (Rhode Island); hoagies (Pennsylvania); hero (New York); poh' boy (Texas).

Schnazzy   Sharp or goodlookin'. Also spiffy.

Scuppernong   Grapes (North Carolina)

Serviette   Napkin

Sweetening, short   Sugar

Sweetening, long   Molasses

Simmer down   Quiet down

Sleep-in   Oversleep (Pittsburgh)

Slippers   Shoes

Slew   Many

Snuff-dipper   Person who uses snuff

Soft drink   Pop; soda; sodie; Coke; tonic (New England)

So long   Goodbye

Sofa   Couch; divan; davenport; chesterfield; settee (South)

Speck not   Probably not

Speck so   Maybe yes

Specs   Eyeglasses

Sprinkling   Equal to a tad

Stars and stripes   Pork and beans eaten cold on Sundays in Boston (1883)

Steppins   Panties; Underwear

Sticks   Rural area

Surface car   Trolley car

Suspeculate   Suspect and speculate simultaneously

Slipperslide   Shoehorn (North Carolina)

Tad   Small amount

Tadpoles   People (Mississippi)

Terrikly   Directly

The thundering heard   A pot of beans (Texas)

Tin Lizzie   Model T Ford

Tissell-Prissell   Scaredy-cat

Toad-floater   Heavy rain

Tol'able   Fairly well (North Carolina)

Tooth carpenter   Maine dentist

To-reckly   Immediately

Tongue bang   To scold someone

City slicker   A visitor from the big city

Traipse   To walk or run

Truck room   Storage room (Pennsylvania Dutch)

Tuckered out   Tired

Tumblings and blankets   Tobacco and paper for making cigarettes

Turtle   One who lacks education

Turtle hull   Trunk of car

Uppity   Having a haughty manner

Warsh   To wash the clothes

Washing powder   Laundry soap

Water fountain   Cooler; bubbler; water barrel (Old English)

One-man band   Wedding ring

We'uns   Us

Window light   Window pane

Wrench   Rinse

Yard birds   Chickens

Yea, bo!   Certainly

You'uns   You people

Young'uns   Kids

Zink   Kitchen sink (Texas)

WRITE YOUR OWN

I'm sure that by now you have thought of a few sayings yourself, or your friends have come up with a few home-spun remarks. The next few pages of *Country Talk* are for you.

Jot down your favorites, and if the mood is just right, send them along to me, so that we can give you credit the next time we come out with a collection of *Country Talk*.

You may send your sayings to:

DICK SYATT
c/o CITADEL PRESS
120 ENTERPRISE AVENUE
SECAUCUS, NEW JERSEY 07094